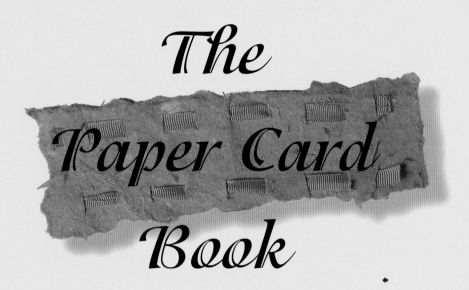

The Paper Card Book

Lisa Kerr

Quarry Books
Rockport, Massachusetts

First published in the United States of America by
Quarry Books, an imprint of
Rockport Publishers, Inc.
146 Granite Street
Rockport, Massachusetts 01966-1299
Telephone: (508) 546-9590
Fax: (508) 546-7141

Distributed to the book trade and art trade in the United States by
North Light Books, an imprint of
F & W Publications
1507 Dana Avenue
Cincinnati, Ohio 45207
Telephone: (800) 289-0963

Other Distribution by
Rockport Publishers, Inc.
Rockport, Massachusetts 01966-1299

ISBN 1-56496-327-6

10 9 8 7 6 5 4 3 2 1

Designer: CopperLeaf, Columbus, Ohio
Cover Photograph: Will Shively, Columbus, Ohio
Photography: Elias Mucarzel
Photograph of author (page 76): Martin Berinstein

Manufactured in Hong Kong by Regent Publishing Services Limited.

A·c·k·n·o·w·l·e·d·g·m·e·n·t·s

One cannot accomplish a task of this size alone. I would like to thank the following people for their collaboration, dedication, and support in making *The Paper Card Book* unfold: Foremost, to Amy Madanick and Casandra McIntyre at Rugg Road Paper Company, Boston, Massachusetts, for not only recommending me to Rockport Publishers, but also for providing me with an abundance of kindness, expertise, and of course, their beautiful papers; to Ann Saydah, my "in-house" editor and dearest friend, whose love and persistence guided me tremendously; to Torri Crowell for lending her graceful hands to every step as well as her warm heart and giving spirit to the book; to Albert Gaucher, who brought beauty and style to the photography and his irresistible charm to the long days; to Serge Dusseault, the Canadian consultant of potato printing with a talent for ideas and inspirations; to Carol Van Heerden for her ingenuity and inspiration where paper, fabric, and thread meet; and to Elias Mucarzel for his photographic skills. Grateful acknowledgement is made to Black Ink for use of their stamp designs in this book.

And lastly, a world of thanks to the staff at Rockport Publishers. Their enthusiasm, guidance, and patience were a great help to me. I would especially like to thank the editor, Martha Wetherill, for her expertise and encouragement; Rosalie Grattaroti for getting the project underway; Shawna Mullen for her conceptual talents; and Lynne Havighurst and Heather Yale for their detailed and delightful design skills.

Contents

I·n·t·r·o·d·u·c·t·i·o·n

My mother recently showed me a few cards that I had made for her in my childhood. They were assembled with pieces of old greeting cards, sprinkled with glitter, and tied together with brightly colored yarns. I laughed at the technique and the prose, but I treasured the sentiment. It was then that I realized how long I have actually been making cards and what compels me to do it. Making a handmade card is a special and perhaps intimate acknowledgment of a friend or a family member, conveying thoughts that are sometimes difficult to say in person. I wouldn't think of actually buying a card because of the pleasure I derive from making a unique one for each person I know.

The projects in this book originated in cards that I have made for my family and friends over time. Every year I am faced with the challenge of coming up with new cards even more exciting than the last to celebrate birthdays, weddings, or baby arrivals, to send sympathy or get-well messages, to say bon voyage, or to just convey good wishes. Each card is designed around a detail about the recipient that makes it fun for both of us. For a knit designer friend, I sewed buttons and fabric into a card. I glued portraits of Frida Kahlo and a Mexican bingo game onto a card to give to a roommate who likes Mexican art.

You can use anything that happens to be at your disposal to make your own cards. Your creations will be original and personal as a result. It took me the better half of a day sitting on a beach in Fiji, sewing shells onto pieces of a cardboard beer box, to make a postcard. Get into the habit of saving things such as museum tickets, cigar rings, stamps, thread, and old calendars. Build a file so you will have interesting things to choose from. I will attempt to glue anything possible to paper. And the post office knows me well in every place I have lived!

Once you collect your materials, all you need to produce your handmade card is the desire to give something a little unusual, something more meaningful than the typical greeting card. In less time than it takes to go to the store and buy a card, you can make one!

M·a·t·e·r·i·a·l·s

Y ou don't need an arsenal of supplies to make the card projects in this book. A few simple items, available at most art or crafts stores, will produce stunning results and can be used for other craft projects as well.

Tools

Polyvinyl acetate glue (PVA glue) is a white glue that dries clear. It will spread easier when diluted with water (use a ratio of four parts glue to one part water, and adjust as necessary), but be careful that it is not too watery or the wetness will damage the paper. Transfer the glue to a plastic container with a lid to make it easier to dilute the glue, and to dip larger brushes into the glue more quickly.

Use inexpensive brushes to apply PVA glue because it can harden and destroy them. Cheap, wooden-handle brushes, in sizes of 1" (2.5 cm) to 2" (5 cm), are available at hardware stores. For smaller tipped brushes, look for sets of children's brushes. To extend the life of your brushes, wash them with hot water after each use and let dry, or leave them in water overnight.

A craft knife is essential for these projects because it gives you control over the edges you wish to create. Buy extra blades and change them often. A metal ruler makes cutting paper much easier. The cork underside of the ruler keeps it from moving, and elevates it to keep the craft knife aligned against the ruler. A self-healing cutting mat protects your work surface from knife cuts, won't slip as you cut, and helps to produce crisp, clean edges in your card projects.

A bone folder is a carved piece of bone or plastic, rounded at one end and pointed at the other, that helps to fold paper. Use the pointed edge to score folds in thick paper, or the round end to smooth out wrinkles after glue has been applied. Be careful not to rub the paper surface too much, or the bone folder will impart a sheen to the paper.

Paper

Today there is a abundance of papers to choose from in a range of prices. Thicker papers, such as handmade or mold-made papers, are better for folding and for serving as the card base. Decorative papers such as marbled, block-printed, silk-screened, or printed papers are ideal for layering onto card bases. Before buying paper for your card base, gently bend, fold, or crease it to see if it will crack along the fold. Some papers have a grain, which is often parallel to the longest dimension of a sheet. Papers fold or tear easily with the direction of the grain.

Decorative Elements

Experiment with grosgrain ribbon, soft satin, or voluptuous velvet to enhance your cards or envelopes. Twine, string, rawhide, gimp, raffia, lace, and woven trims add texture and dimension. Tie, weave, or sew them by hand or machine.

Collect old buttons from yard sales and flea markets. Kitchen supply stores are filled with cake-decorating treasures to adorn your cards. Look for shells and dried flowers on your next trip to the beach or woods. Ask family and friends to save stamps from foreign countries for your collage collection. And tell them to save last year's calendars to tear up for collage elements or fold into handmade envelopes.

Look for printing inks in art supply stores. I prefer water-based inks because they are easy to clean, take less time to dry, and are very vibrant. The rubber ink roller or brayer is a fairly inexpensive tool that you will use often. You can print from any object with a relief surface, from vegetables to keys, Styrofoam, or coins.

You will need photo corners for a few of the projects. Traditional black corners lend an air of antiquity to your design, but white photo corners and self-adhesive clear corners are also available at paper specialty stores and office supply stores.

C·o·l·l·a·g·e C·a·r·d·s

*U*sing your imagination—and a little glue—you can create a card featuring a paper collage customized for any occasion. Collage combines texture, color, and shape to achieve a balanced visual presentation. The colors, patterns, and textures of your papers will inspire the basic design. Enhance the card with objects from your everyday travels or color photocopies of your favorite images, photographs, or postcards to add a personal touch. For a travel theme, incorporate maps, stamps, and postcards. Use dried flowers and handmade papers for a soft, natural effect. To add texture and to achieve a festive feeling, weave ribbon through slits in the card. Layer papers to create a multipaged card that holds a special message in the innermost layer. The possibilities are almost endless and depend on the occasion, the recipient, and the materials you have available.

Collage Card Inspirations

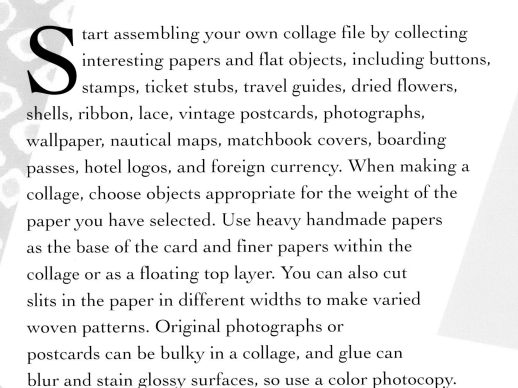

S tart assembling your own collage file by collecting interesting papers and flat objects, including buttons, stamps, ticket stubs, travel guides, dried flowers, shells, ribbon, lace, vintage postcards, photographs, wallpaper, nautical maps, matchbook covers, boarding passes, hotel logos, and foreign currency. When making a collage, choose objects appropriate for the weight of the paper you have selected. Use heavy handmade papers as the base of the card and finer papers within the collage or as a floating top layer. You can also cut slits in the paper in different widths to make varied woven patterns. Original photographs or postcards can be bulky in a collage, and glue can blur and stain glossy surfaces, so use a color photocopy.

Weave dried flower stems, paper strips, fabric, plastic, wood, or wire through slits in your card.

A n easy way to get started is to buy pre-cut blank cards. These can be found at stationery or art supply stores. You will have a larger selection of color and textured papers, however, if you create your own card base from the paper you have on hand.

Travel Collage

Collect items related to a destination. Arrange the collage pieces first to help determine the color and weight of the paper. Begin with more collage elements than you may actually use. Glue the smaller elements together before attaching them to the card. Pick coordinating colors from the map to use for the collage papers. Center the background paper and map on the card. Then layer the torn paper and photo, followed by the stamps and travel motif.

Materials

- Piece of heavyweight paper, 10" x 7" (25 cm x 18 cm), folded in half
- Piece of background paper, 3" x 5" (8 cm x 13 cm)
- Piece of map, 2" x 4" (5 cm x 10 cm)
- Piece of decorative paper, torn to 4½" x 1" (11 cm x 2.5 cm)
- Two postage stamps
- Color photocopy of a postcard, magazine, or photographic image, 2" x 1" (5 cm x 2.5 cm)
- Travel motif (i.e., suitcase, airplane, train, building, statue)
- Craft knife
- Metal ruler
- PVA glue
- Glue brush
- Cutting mat

❖**1** Apply glue with a brush to the back of the background paper, stroking from the center of the paper out to the edges. Do not use too much glue or it will wrinkle and stain the card. Adhere each layer to the card firmly before applying the next layer.

❖*2* Center the background paper on the heavyweight paper with a 1" (2.5 cm) border on all sides, and adhere it to the front of the card. Place the paper down gently at first in case you need to adjust it. Press the paper flat with your fingers, starting at the center and moving out to the edges.

❖*3* Apply glue to the back of the map. Center it on the background paper, and adhere it. To avoid bubbling, press the paper down from the center out to the edges.

❖*4* Apply glue in a band that is approximately ⅛" (.3 cm) wide to the front left side of the postcard, magazine, or photographic image. Adhere the image to the center of the right side of the torn paper strip to create a unit.

❖*5* Apply glue to the back of the torn paper strip and postcard, magazine, or photographic image. Cover the entire surface, including the edges. Center the unit and adhere it to the map, so that the top and bottom edges of the torn paper extend beyond the map.

❖*6* Apply glue to the back of the travel motif, and adhere it to the center of the torn paper strip, overlapping the postcard, magazine, or photographic image.

❖*7* Apply glue to the back of the stamps. Position one at the top left corner of the map, overlapping the torn paper and the edge of the map. Place the other at the lower left corner of the map on top of the torn paper. Make sure all edges of both stamps are firmly glued.

Dried Flower Collage

Handcrafted papers made with dried herbs and flowers are ideal for this project because the texture is as important as the collage elements. Apply two textured papers to a base card, add roses, scent the card with rose oil, and send it to a friend. Wrapping the finished card in tissue or lightweight paper protects the flowers and adds a nice surprise when the envelope is opened.

Materials
- Piece of handmade paper with pressed flowers or leaves, 8" x 6" (20 cm x 15 cm), folded in half
- Two pieces of textured paper, 3 ½" x 4" (8.5 cm x 10 cm) and 1 ¾" x 4 ½" (4.5 cm x 11 cm)
- Miniature dried roses or other small dried flowers
- Craft knife
- Metal ruler
- PVA glue
- Glue brush
- Cutting mat

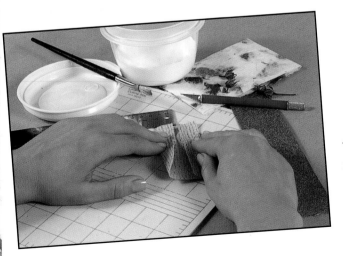

❖**1** Lay the piece of 3 ½" x 4" (9 cm x 10 cm) textured paper flat on the work surface. Measure ¾" (2 cm) from the left edge and make a fold. Measure ¾" (2 cm) from the right edge and make a fold.

❖2 Apply glue to the back of the textured paper in the center panel only (between the folds). Be careful not to apply glue over the folded edges, as it will show on the finished side of the panel.

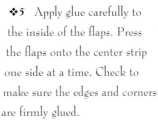

❖3 Center the panel on the front of the card and adhere it. Press firmly along the folded edges to create a flap on each side. If any of the flowers in the handmade paper fall off, stick them back on with a dab of glue.

❖4 Create a ragged edge on each end of the strip of 1 ¾" x 4 ½" (4.5 cm x 11 cm) textured paper by tearing no more than ¼" (.5 cm) from the top and bottom edges. Glue this strip inside the panel on top of the card.

❖5 Apply glue carefully to the inside of the flaps. Press the flaps onto the center strip one side at a time. Check to make sure the edges and corners are firmly glued.

❖6 Apply a small dab of glue to a flower and gently place it on the center strip. Hold the flower with your finger for a minute until the glue sets. Space the flowers evenly down the center strip. Dried flowers are brittle and often crumble, so handle them gently and always have a few more than you think you need.

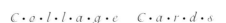

Woven Ribbon Collage

Create an elegant card by weaving paper and ribbon. Use stiff paper so the card will not sag from the weight of the ribbon. Cut slits in the card using the ribbon and paper strips as a guide. Weave the ribbon and paper strips through the slits, and glue the paper to the back of the card. Add a surprise by tying the ribbon in a bow.

Materials

- Piece of heavyweight or printmaking paper, 6" x 8" (15 cm x 20 cm), folded in half
- Piece of ½" to 1" (1 cm to 2.5 cm) cloth ribbon, 30" (76 cm) long
- Assorted handmade paper scraps, ¾" x 7" (2 cm x 18 cm) each
- Masking tape
- Pin, push pin, or sewing needle
- Craft knife with extra blades
- Metal ruler
- Pencil
- PVA glue
- Glue brush
- Cutting mat

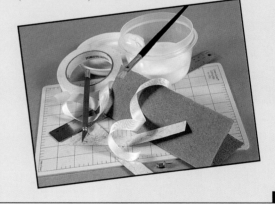

❖1 Open the card flat and secure the edges with masking tape. Lay the ribbon horizontally across the middle of the card. Tape one end of the ribbon to the work surface. Pull it taut to make it straight, then tape the other end. Using a pin to mark the distance, measure ½" (1 cm) in from both sides of the card along the top and bottom edges of the ribbon. From those points, measure and mark four 1" (2.5 cm) intervals along the edges of the ribbon.

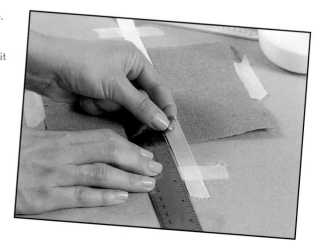

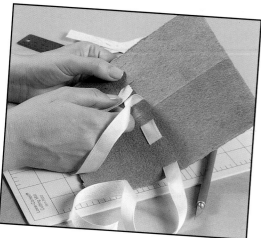

❖*2* Carefully remove the tape and the ribbon. Place the card flat on the cutting mat. With the metal ruler, align the pin holes vertically. Slowly cut slits from top to bottom, using the tip of the craft knife along the edge of the ruler. For clean, precise slits, use a new blade. Cut both ends of the ribbon on a diagonal. Use one end to thread the ribbon through the slits.

❖*3* Place the card on your work surface. Measure ½" (1 cm) above and below the edges of the ribbon. Mark the spots lightly with the pencil. Place two ¾" (2 cm) paper strips horizontally on the ½" (1 cm) marks above and below the ribbon. Secure the ends with tape so the strips will not move.

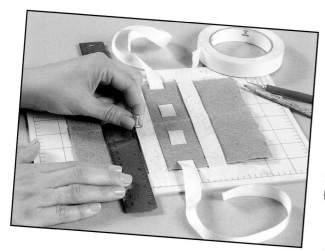

❖*4* Measure and mark with the pin 1" (2.5 cm) from the right edge of the card at the top and bottom edges of the paper strips. Then make holes at ½" (1 cm) intervals along the edges of the paper strips only as far as the folded edge of the card.

❖*5* Remove the tape and the paper strips. Open the card flat on the cutting mat. With the metal ruler, align the pin holes vertically. Slowly cut slits from top to bottom, using the tip of the craft knife along the edge of the ruler.

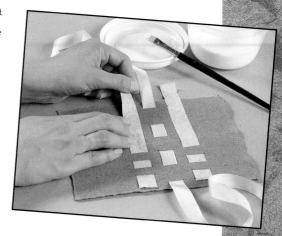

❖*6* Weave the paper strips through the slits above and below the ribbon. The edges of the paper strips should extend about ¼" to ½" (.5 cm to 1 cm) beyond the front right edge of the card. Apply glue to the back of the paper strips from the fold to the left edge of the card. Be careful not to apply glue beyond the edge of the card because that piece of the strip will hang over the edge of the card. Adhere the strips to the back of the card.

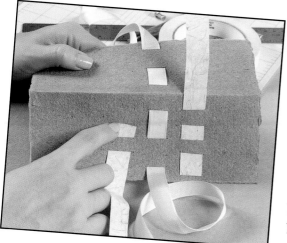

Lavishly Layered Card

This design highlights the beauty of handmade paper. Use four different textures or colors to create a theme. Cut the papers to different sizes, fold them, and bind them together. Do not make the holes on the fold too large or the layers will be loose. If the ribbon is too wide, fold it in half lengthwise and use pliers to pull it through. Complete the card by writing a special message on the innermost page or even a single word on every layer.

Materials

- Piece of handmade flower paper, torn to 8 ½" x 5 ¾" (21 cm x 14.5 cm)
- Piece of heavyweight or printmaking paper, 9" x 6 ¼" (23 cm x 16 cm)
- Piece of colored lace paper, 8" x 5" (20 cm x 13 cm)
- Piece of handmade or textured writing paper, torn or cut to 4" x 7" (10 cm x 18 cm)
- Cord, string, or thin ribbon for binding
- Toothpick, knitting needle, or awl
- Craft knife
- Metal ruler
- Pencil
- Bone folder
- Cutting mat

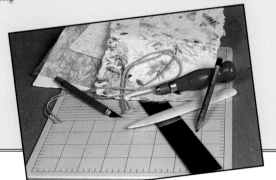

❖1 Fold each paper in half separately in the following way: Take the top left corner of the paper and fold it over to the top right corner, matching the corner edges exactly; holding the edges together with your right hand, make a small crease at the top left edge with your left hand; press with your thumb firmly to crease the fold. If any edges are not even, carefully trim them with the ruler and knife.

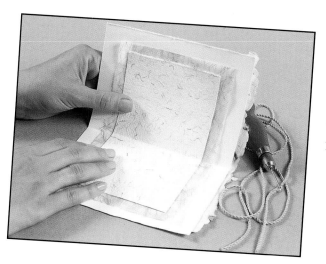

❖2 Lay the 8 ½" x 5 ¾" (21.5 cm x 14.5 cm) handmade paper flat on the work surface. Place the 9" x 6 ¼" (23 cm x 16 cm) sturdy paper on top of it. Center the 8" x 5" (20 cm x 13 cm) lace paper on top of the sturdy paper. Then center the 4" x 7" (10 cm x 18 cm) handmade paper on top of the lace paper. Stack the fold lines directly on top of each other.

❖3 Open all the layers, center them, and hold them in place. From the top of the outermost paper, measure 2" (5 cm) down the card on the fold line and mark lightly with the pencil. From the bottom of the outermost paper, measure 2" (5 cm) up the card on the fold line and mark lightly with the pencil.

❖4 Fold the card halfway shut, holding all the layers together. With the sharp tool (toothpick, knitting needle, or awl), puncture a small hole through the marks on the fold line. Make sure you go through all the layers before you remove the tool.

❖5 Thread the ribbon through the holes, starting from the inside of the card. Use the sharp object to help thread it through. Tie the ribbon in a knot or bow along the spine of the card.

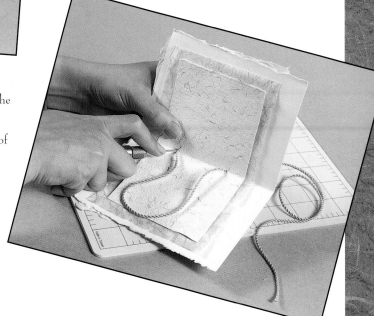

P·r·i·n·t·e·d C·a·r·d·s

Yo do not need to be an artist or know sophisticated printing methods to make these ingenious printed cards. Just combine a selection of easy-to-make printed images, papers, and fabrics to create thank-you notes, birthday cards, gift enclosures, or invitations. For an elegant card, apply rubber stamps to fabric. Cut your own shapes from potatoes and print cards with these stamps for a playful, organic look. If you cannot draw, photocopying your favorite images onto transparent film is a wonderful way to make cards. Take advantage of this process to include type on your card as well: type or print a name, add an image, and photocopy it onto film. Then make a window in your card and insert the transparency. Your friends and family will delight in receiving unique, personalized printed cards.

P·r·i·n·t·e·d C·a·r·d
I·n·s·p·i·r·a·t·i·o·n·s

L ook to common materials you have at home—leaves, feathers, textured wood, coins, keys, flattened tin cans, Styrofoam, rubber tires, or any object with a flat relief surface. Also try making stamps from vegetables other than potatoes, such as sliced mushrooms or bell peppers. You can design different stamped projects, such as wrapping paper, napkins, tablecloths, gift tags, or labels. Stamp images onto smaller pieces of rice paper and incorporate them into a collage. Personalize your cards and invitations with transparent film.

Make your own stamps by cutting designs into rubber erasers.

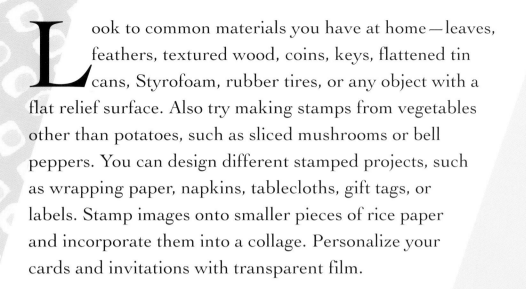

U se easy-to-clean water-based paints. You can also use tempera or acrylic paint.

Tear the paper for a softer edge. Fold it back and forth a few times before tearing. For a rectangular shape, tear it against the edge of a metal ruler. For a free-form shape, tear it with your hands.

Rubber Stamp Card

Cut a window for your stamped image in the front of the card. Stamp the image onto sheer fabric, placing a piece of scrap paper under the fabric to keep the ink from bleeding through. Let the ink dry. Glue gold paper on the inside of the card under the stamped fabric. Sew the buttons on to fasten the fabric to the card, and then fray the edges of the fabric.

Materials

- Piece of fibrous handmade paper, cut or torn to 8" x 4 ½" (20 cm x 11.5 cm) and folded in half
- Piece of sheer fabric (polyester or silk organza), 2" x 3" (5 cm x 7.5 cm)
- Piece of gold or decorative paper, cut or torn to 2" x 2 ½" (5 cm x 6.5 cm)
- Rubber stamp with an image not larger than 1 ½" (4 cm)
- Ink pad with dark ink
- Needle and thread or sewing machine
- Two small, flat buttons
- Craft knife
- Metal ruler
- Pencil
- PVA glue
- Glue brush
- Bone folder
- Cutting mat
- Scrap paper

❖1 Lay the folded handmade paper on your work surface and measure and mark 1 ¼" (3 cm) from the middle of the top and bottom edges. Then measure and mark 1 ½" (4 cm) from the middle of the left and right edges. Open the card flat on the cutting mat. Cut through the marks, angling the knife to make an oval hole approximately 1 ½" x 1" (4 cm x 2.5 cm) in the center of the card. Erase any pencil marks left on the card.

❖*2* Trace the shape of the hole onto the scrap paper. To determine exactly where to stamp the image on the fabric, center the fabric over the traced hole.

❖*3* Place the rubber stamp on the ink pad and tap gently two or three times. Press the stamp flat onto the fabric, applying an even amount of pressure on all sides. Be careful not to rock the stamp from side to side, as this will cause the ink to smear. Lift the stamp straight up from the fabric. Let the ink dry before attaching the fabric to the card.

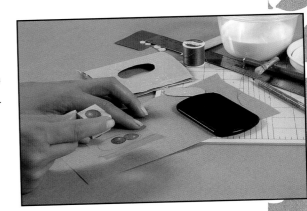

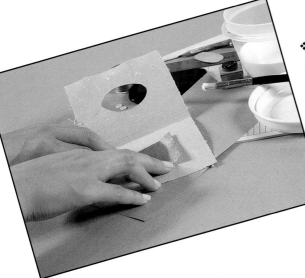

❖*4* Open the card. Apply glue to the back of the gold paper. Center the paper behind the oval cutout on the front of the card, and adhere it to the inside of the card. It is best to use gold, silver, or light-colored papers for the background to the stamped fabric—stamped images tend to disappear against a dark background.

❖*5* Center the stamped fabric over the hole on the front of the card. Sew the buttons above and below the oval to secure the fabric to the paper. Fray the edges of the fabric to create a frame around the oval.

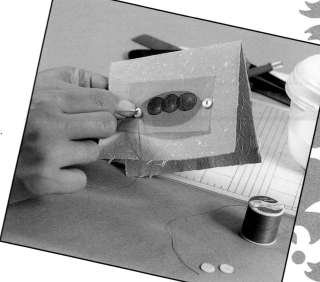

Potato Print Card

To create a star stamp, make a cutting guide by tracing the shape of the potato and drawing a star, or by pressing a cookie cutter star into the potato. Cut out around the star. Let the potato sit face down on a paper towel to drain for fifteen minutes before printing. Tap the stamp in ink on an inking slab or roll ink onto the relief surface. Then stamp the card. Repeat or overlap the stamps to make a pattern.

Materials

- Washed and uncooked large, firm potato
- Piece of heavyweight or printmaking paper, 10" x 7" (25 cm x 18 cm), folded in half
- Tracing or scrap paper
- Craft or paring knife
- Pins
- Scissors
- Metal ruler
- Pencil
- One or two colors of water-soluble printing inks
- Rubber ink roller
- Inking slab (smooth, nonabsorbent, easy-to-clean surface such as glass, sheet metal, plastic, or Formica)

❖1 Cut the potato in half. To make a pattern for your stamp, place the cut edge of the potato on the tracing or scrap paper. Use the pencil to trace the shape of the potato. You can also cut the potato freehand—experiment with different shapes.

❖*2* Make a five-point star in the paper circle; simple shapes are easier to execute than intricate patterns. Mark the pieces you will cut away with an X. Cut out the circle using the scissors.

❖*3* Pin the paper pattern to the surface of the potato in the spaces marked with an X. Use the knife to cut away the five marked sections of the potato. For the best results, cut from the center of the potato out to the edge, approximately ½" (1 cm) deep, then along the side of the potato. Cut straight up and down in one motion, and clean any loose edges with your knife, as they will appear in the printed image.

❖*4* Squeeze a dollop of ink onto the inking slab. Use the rubber roller to spread the ink to a thin consistency. You can roll two colors side by side, but be sure to wash the roller before changing colors to avoid mixing ink colors.

❖*5* To ink the stamp, tap the potato a few times on the freshly spread ink or run the roller over the relief image. Wash the stamp before changing colors to avoid mixing ink colors. Be sure to cover the entire surface of the potato with ink, filling in any blank spots with your finger.

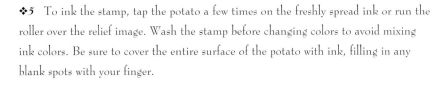

❖*6* Use both hands to press the stamp firmly onto the paper. Be careful not to smudge the ink. Lift the stamp up and away from the paper. If the potato print is watery, stamp the potato a few times on scrap paper before re-inking. Reapply ink to the stamp each time you print.

Transparent Film Card

Rummage through books for images you would like to use, or make an original drawing. For the best results, select images printed in black, such as old playing cards, etching plates from an opera libretto, and mod Japanese graphic design images. Photocopy the images onto transparent film or acetate; reproduction businesses provide this service for a small fee. Then cut the paper for the card and background papers to place behind the image. Assemble the card with brass fasteners.

Materials

- Transparent film with photocopied image
- Piece of Japanese handmade paper, 8" x 5" (20 cm x 13 cm), folded in half
- Piece of medium-weight cardstock for the inside, 7 ½" x 4 ½" (19 cm x 11.5 cm)
- Piece of background paper, 2 ¾" x 3 ½" (7 cm x 9 cm)
- Piece of gold or silver paper
- Brass paper fasteners (found in stationery stores)
- Craft knife
- Metal ruler
- PVA glue
- Glue brush
- Cutting mat

❖**1** Place the folded card on the work surface. Apply glue to the back of the background paper. Center the background paper and adhere it to the front of the card. Adhere the other layers of paper you will use as a backdrop for the acetate image. Use gold, silver, or light-colored background paper to enhance the image.

❖2 Open the card. Align the fold of the inside paper with the fold of the base card. Position the papers as they will appear in the finished card.

❖3 Position the acetate image on the front of the card over the background papers. With the knife, cut a small slit in the upper left corner through the acetate and all the layers of paper. Be careful not to scrape the transparent film or acetate, because the image may flake off or become damaged.

❖4 Slide the brass fastener through the slit. You could also attach the acetate by sewing it to the paper, or using clear picture corners to hold the image.

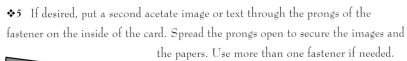

❖5 If desired, put a second acetate image or text through the prongs of the fastener on the inside of the card. Spread the prongs open to secure the images and the papers. Use more than one fastener if needed.

Variation
If you don't have any brass fasteners on hand, attach the acetate to the paper by sliding it into four slits cut into the card, as shown in this variation.

F·o·l·d-o·u·t C·a·r·d·s

These cards present a magical message through a series of accordion folds, transcending the expected two-sided card by adding depth to your design. Whether you make four folds or fifteen, the playful suspense of unfolding a card is delightful. The technique of folding can easily be mastered with just a little practice. Fold a diagonal shape to create a simple card with clean lines. Cut the diagonal in a wave pattern for a softer effect. For a sturdy fold-out card, cover a board and decorate the cover with buttons or beads. Play with the space: write a single line across the middle of the card or one word in each layer. From two sheets of paper, fashion a surprising folded square with a special greeting or photograph inside. Fold-out cards can be startling or mysterious, sophisticated or playful—and they are always special.

F·o·l·d-o·u·t C·a·r·d I·n·s·p·i·r·a·t·i·o·n·s

D esign a fold-out birthday card that has a panel for each year to be celebrated. These elongated cards can also be used to send a poem or write a letter. Use pinking shears to create a zigzag edge, or sew a pattern on the diagonal edge with embroidery thread. Run a gold marker along the edge to highlight the shape. Add a third dimension to your card by gluing objects onto the inner fold that pop up when the card is opened. Announce a birth or congratulate a graduate with a personalized message in a surprising folded square.

Make a miniature art gallery by putting a photo or collage in each panel.

M ark the paper carefully and fold it accurately the first time. Refolding leaves unwanted lines. Practice on a piece of scrap paper first.

Some papers are not suitable for writing, so select a paper with a smooth surface and test it with your pen before you write the final copy.

Classic Fold-out Card

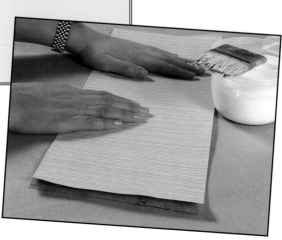

Classic lines and contrasting papers make this card striking. The construction is simple, with the different papers folded on top of each other in a diagonal line. Cut the papers, glue them together, and fold. Try a pattern and a solid color together or two solid colors. Personalize your card with words or images. You can also make this card with one sheet of paper, but adhering two sheets makes the card sturdier and the design more interesting.

Materials

- Two pieces of paper in contrasting colors and textures 7 ½" x 20 ½" (19 cm x 52 cm) each
- Craft knife
- Metal ruler
- Pencil
- PVA glue
- Glue brush
- Bone folder

❖1 Apply glue to one sheet of paper. Align the edges and adhere the glued piece to the other sheet of paper. Smooth the papers with your hands to press out any wrinkles. Trim the edges to 7" x 20" (18 cm x 51 cm).

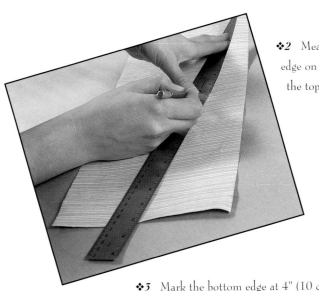

❖*2*   Measure and mark with the pencil 3 ½" (9 cm) up from the bottom edge on the right side of the paper. Cut the top edge in a diagonal from the top left corner to the 3 ½" (9 cm) mark on the right side.

❖*3*   Mark the bottom edge at 4" (10 cm) intervals to indicate the fold lines. Fold the left edge in along the first fold line. Align the top edge of the paper with the edge underneath for a straight fold line.

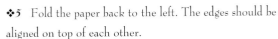

❖*4*   Turn the paper over. Fold the paper back, align it with the bottom edge underneath, and crease the paper with your thumb or the bone folder.

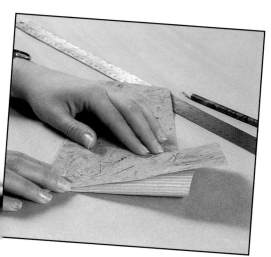

❖*5*   Fold the paper back to the left. The edges should be aligned on top of each other.

❖*6*   Fold the last flap to the right. Crease all the folds with the bone folder for a crisp fold. Trim any excess paper. To personalize the card, glue decorative paper or images to the front of the card.

Accordion Fold Card

Be the master of many folds. Cover two pieces of illustration board with decorative paper. This provides a protective case for the folded paper inside and is also sturdy enough for attaching beads or buttons. Glue the paper to be folded to the inside of one board, then fold it an even number of intervals to achieve the accordion effect. You can make more than four folds but, to ensure the card folds properly, remember to use an even number of folds.

Materials

- Two pieces of illustration board, 4" x 4" (10 cm x 10 cm)
- Two pieces of decorative paper for the outside, 5" x 5" (13 cm x 13 cm)
- Piece of text paper for the inside, 3 ¾" x 15 ½" (9.5 cm x 39 cm)
- Metal ruler
- Pencil
- PVA glue
- Glue brush
- Bone folder

❖**1** On the back of one piece of the 5" x 5" (13 cm x 13 cm) decorative paper, measure and mark ½" (1 cm) from the edge on all sides. Apply glue within the lines. Center one piece of illustration board on the paper. Turn the card over and use your hand to smooth the paper from the center to the edges.

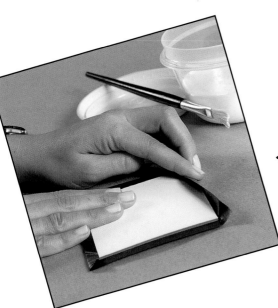

*Always work in a clean
area, with scrap paper
under your projects.*

❖2 Turn the card over again. Apply glue to the right and left flaps
with the brush. Fold the flaps over the illustration board and smooth
them with your fingers. Do not press the paper together at the top
and bottom of the flaps where the paper extends beyond the board;
the corners are handled in the next step.

❖3 Apply glue to the flaps at the top corners. In each corner,
pull the top piece of folded paper to a 45-degree angle and crease.
Angle the fold so the paper will not hang over the edges of the board.
Tuck any excess paper toward the edge of the board. Repeat on the
bottom corners.

❖4 Apply glue to the top and bottom flaps and fold them
onto the board. Make sure that the angled corners are attached
to the inside edge of the board or you will see them on the
outside of the card when it is closed. Repeat steps 1 through
4 for the other side of the cover.

❖5 Center the inside paper ¼" (.5 cm) from the top, bottom, and left edges of one board. Make a fold in the paper ¼" (.5 cm) from the right edge of the board. Make sure, as you fold, to align the folded paper on top of the bottom portion of the paper.

❖6 Turn the paper over. Apply glue from the fold line to the edge of the paper. Center the paper and adhere it to the board ¼" (.5 cm) from the edges. Let the glue dry for a few minutes, then fold the paper to the left. Crease the fold with a bone folder.

Be careful not to glue beyond the fold line on the inside paper, as it will show on the finished card.

❖7 Make a fold along the left edge of the paper, starting at the top left corner. Align the fold with the left edge of the paper on the board underneath.

❖8 Slide the board under the paper beside the other board to use as a guide for paper placement. Turn the folded paper and glued board over, and apply glue from the last fold line to the outside edge.

❖9 Center the paper and adhere it to the second board ¼" (.5 cm) from the right edge. Smooth the paper with your fingers and with the bone folder. Align the boards on top of each other at the right edge, and press down evenly toward the left edge.

Variation

A smaller card, with more folds and shapes cut from the folded inside paper, adds light and shadow to the greeting.

Surprising Square Card

The Surprising Square is perfect to give as an invitation or graduation card. Words of welcome or congratulations surprise and delight as they emerge from colorful layers of paper. The challenge of this card is in the alignment; it may take a few attempts to get it right. Use black, red, and gold paper to make a traditional Japanese card. Cover the card in layers of tissue for a softer feeling, or clear patterned acetate or plastic wrapping paper for a more sophisticated message.

Materials

- Piece of patterned paper, 10" x 10" (25 cm x 25 cm)
- Piece of solid color paper, 10" x 10" (25 cm x 25 cm)
- Piece of card stock or heavy paper, 4" x 4" (10 cm x 10 cm)
- Strip of paper for closure, 11 ¼" x 1 ½" (28.5 cm x 4 cm)
- Craft knife
- Double stick tape
- PVA glue
- Glue brush
- Metal ruler
- Bone folder

❖*1* Position the two sheets of 10" x 10" (25 cm x 25 cm) paper back to back with the wrong sides together. Align the edges. Fix the papers in place with a piece of double stick tape. Trim the edges if they aren't even.

❖*2* Turn the paper on a diagonal. Measure and mark 4 ¾" (12 cm) intervals along the vertical, dividing the paper into three parts. Use the metal ruler and bone folder to score horizontal lines at the marked intervals.

Fold along the edge of a ruler for clean lines.

❖*3* Fold the paper on the bottom score line. Then fold the point back down evenly to the bottom edge. The point should meet the edge of the bottom fold. Crease the folds with the bone folder.

❖*4* Fold the paper on the top score line. Then fold the point back to the upper edge. Use the bottom point fold as a guide. The folds should be flush with one another. Crease the folds with the bone folder.

❖5   Score the horizontal lines at each
end of the folded triangles to make the
square shape.

*For best results, measure
twice and cut accurately.*

❖6   Fold the left flap in. Align
the left and right edges with the
edges underneath for an even
square. Fold the flap point back to
the left edge. Crease well.

❖7   Repeat the last two folds on the
right side.

❖8 Insert the 4" x 4" (10 cm x 10 cm) message
card or a photograph inside.

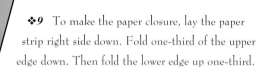

❖9 To make the paper closure, lay the paper
strip right side down. Fold one-third of the upper
edge down. Then fold the lower edge up one-third.

❖10 Wrap the paper strip around the card so
that the edges of the strip meet evenly on one side. Apply glue to the
lower half of the strip and press the strip ends together. The band
should be able to slide on and off easily.

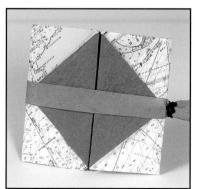

*For a different closure, wrap
thread several times around
the end of the paper bands.
Trim ends.*

Variations

*Experiment with different
papers and patterns, to
dramatically alter the square
design. Try centering strong
geometric patterns them on the
square shape. Or mix the pale
pastels of old maps with darker,
solid colors.*

*A*lthough photo mailers appear complicated, they are easy to make; think of them as paper packages holding wonderful images inside. This unique style of card works as both a card and a photograph frame. Small photo mailers are perfect as baby announcements and can be made to the size of any picture. Tailor this card to many different occasions by choosing various papers. Do not limit yourself to photographs when designing a photo mailer. Window photo mailers take a little more work to construct, but can be used to frame small three-dimensional items, such as seashells, keys, or dried flowers, depending on the occasion.

P·h·o·t·o M·a·i·l·e·r
I·n·s·p·i·r·a·t·i·o·n·s

☺ You will have gold pieces by the bushel.

LA MANO

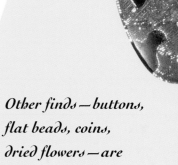

U se festive paper to create a birthday theme, or white and gold papers for an elegant wedding invitation. Decorate the cover of the photo mailer with a collage, special mementos, or images cut from books and magazines. You can build a paper "inspirations" file by collecting everyday items such as stamps, photographs, ticket stubs, playbills, subway maps, wine labels (especially exotic ones), cookie fortunes, travel brochures, road maps, shopping bags, and calendars.

Other finds — buttons, flat beads, coins, dried flowers — are treasures that can double as decorations.

P aper selection is important, especially if you are working with glue for the first time. Thin paper, such as pages from a magazine or wrapping paper, may curl or wrinkle; thick handmade papers will be difficult to work with at the corners. Choose medium-weight papers, such as marbled, Japanese, paste paper, or printed paper.

Mourvèdre

Basic Photo Mailer

This special card combines many of the techniques already presented in the previous chapters. Prepare all the materials before you start to glue. Choose papers for the outside of the cover, the interior, and the binding strip. Measure the papers and then cut out each piece. Once the first few steps have been completed, the corners require special attention. You may want to practice making them a few times before attempting the final project.

Materials

- Two pieces of illustration board, 4" x 6" (10 cm x 15 cm)
- Two pieces of decorative paper for the outside, 5" x 7" (13 cm x 18 cm)
- Two pieces of decorative paper for the inside, 3 ¾" x 5 ¾" (9.5 cm x 14.5 cm)
- Piece of paper for the binding strip (use the same paper as on the inside),
        1 ¼" x 6" (3 cm x 15 cm)
- Piece of writing paper or a photograph, 3 ½" x 5 ½" (9 cm x 14 cm)
- Black photo corners
- Craft knife
- Metal ruler
- Pencil
- PVA glue
- Glue brush
- Bone folder
- Cutting mat

❖*1* Lay the paper for the outside cover pattern-side down. Measure ½" (1 cm) from all edges and mark this border with the pencil. Apply glue to cover the square area inside the pencil lines, then center the illustration board and gently adhere it to the glued surface, using the pencil marks as a guide.

❖*2* Turn the glued piece over. With the side of your thumb or the bone folder, press firmly from the center out to the edges to create a smooth surface. Rub the entire surface with your fingers until the paper is flat and wrinkle-free.

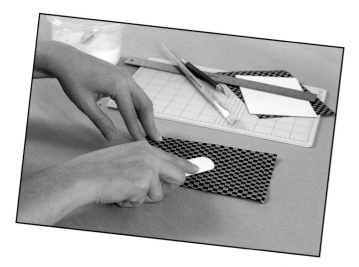

❖*3* Turn the card back over. Apply glue to the long flaps of paper on the right and left edges. Fold the flaps firmly over the illustration board and smooth them with your thumb or the bone folder. Press the paper flat only to the top and bottom edges of the illustration board. Be careful not to press the paper together at the corners where it extends beyond the board.

❖*4* Apply glue to the top corners of the paper. Fold the corner paper at a 45-degree angle toward the center of the board. Crease the paper and press down. Press in the excess paper created by the angle fold along the top edge of the illustration board. Repeat with the bottom corners.

❖5 Apply glue to the remaining short strips of paper at the top and bottom edges of the boards. Fold them over the illustration board and smooth them with a bone folder or your fingers. Make sure that the paper does not hang over the edge of the board.

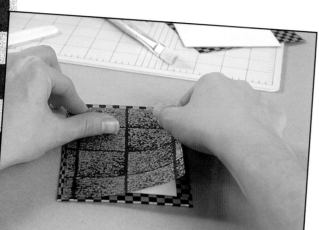

❖6 Apply glue to the back of the contrasting paper. Work from the center out, covering the entire surface and all edges. Center the paper on the illustration board and press to adhere. One half of the card is now complete. Repeat steps 1 through 6 to make the other side of the card.

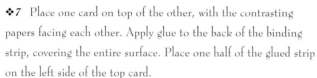

To prevent the illustration board from warping as the glue dries, put a sheet of paper between the sides of the finished card so they will not stick to each other, and press the card under a pile of heavy books.

❖7 Place one card on top of the other, with the contrasting papers facing each other. Apply glue to the back of the binding strip, covering the entire surface. Place one half of the glued strip on the left side of the top card.

❖8 Stand the card upright on its right edge. Square the covers, matching the edges evenly all the way around. Use your thumb and forefinger to roll the binding strip firmly around the two boards to the back card.

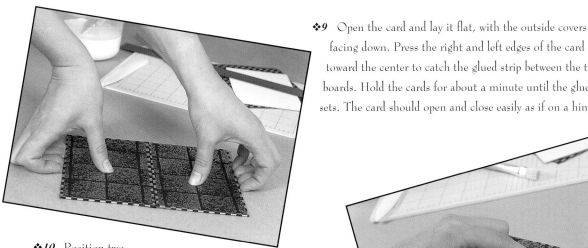

❖9 Open the card and lay it flat, with the outside covers facing down. Press the right and left edges of the card toward the center to catch the glued strip between the two boards. Hold the cards for about a minute until the glue sets. The card should open and close easily as if on a hinge.

❖10 Position two photo corners on the left and right top corners of the 3 ½" x 5 ½" (9 cm x 14 cm) paper. Apply glue to the back of the corners. Press the corners onto the inside of the card at an equal distance from the top edges. Slide the paper out and repeat this procedure with the bottom corners. If you want a double frame, apply corners to the other side of the card as well.

❖11 Insert a 3 ½" x 5 ½" (9 cm x 14 cm) piece of writing paper or photograph into the photo corners to complete your card. To personalize the card, make a paper or photo collage on the front cover with items from your collage file.

Variation

Choose paper to complement the photograph you want to send. Dress up a child's photo with playful, colorful papers from different countries and glue tiny toys or objects to the front of the card.

Baby Photo Mailer

The baby photo mailer is a perfect card to welcome a little one into the world, but this type of card can be used for any occasion. Select papers and ribbon appropriate for your design, and cut them to the required sizes. Glue the paper to the boards, add the ribbon, and bind the boards together. For a double frame, you can apply picture corners on both sides of the card.

Materials

- Two pieces of illustration board or cardboard, 3" x 3" (7.5 cm x 7.5 cm)
- Two pieces of decorative paper for the outside, 4" x 4" (10 cm x 10 cm)
- Two pieces of contrasting decorative paper for the inside, 2 ¾" x 2 ¾" (7 cm x 7 cm)
- Piece of paper for the binding strip (use the same paper as on the inside),
    1" x 3" (2.5 cm x 7.5 cm)
- Piece of writing paper, 2 ½" x 2 ½" (6.5 cm x 6.5 cm)
- Length of ribbon, 8 ½" (21 cm)
- Picture corners
- Craft knife
- Metal ruler
- Pencil
- PVA glue
- Glue brush
- Bone folder
- Cutting mat

❖*1* Apply glue to the back of the paper for the outside cover. Center the illustration board on the paper, leaving approximately ½" (1 cm) on all sides. Turn the card over. Use your fingers to smooth the paper over the board. Start at the center and work out to the edges.

Brush the glue evenly, taking care not to use too much because it will cause the paper to tear, especially in the corners. Also, if the glue leaks out, it will stain the ribbon and paper.

❖*2* Turn the card over again. Apply glue to the right and left flaps. Fold the flaps over the illustration board and smooth the paper with your fingers. Do not press the paper at the top and bottom edges together; they will be folded at an angle for the corners in the next step.

❖*3* Apply glue to the top corner flaps. For each corner, pull the top piece of folded paper to a 45-degree angle. It is important to angle the fold so that the paper will not hang over the edge. Tuck any excess paper toward the board edge. Repeat on the bottom corners.

❖*4* Apply glue to the top and bottom flaps and adhere them to the board. Make sure that the folded corner is glued on the inside of the board edge. Now repeat steps 1 through 4 for the other side of the card.

❖5   Lay the card pieces side by side with the outside covers facing down. Cut the ribbon in half, and add glue to one of the pieces of ribbon, ¼" (.5 cm) away from its end. Glue the ribbon to the middle of the outside edge of one card. To position the ribbon in the same place on the other card, close the card, lay the second piece on top of the first, and make a mark. Glue the second length of ribbon to the other card.

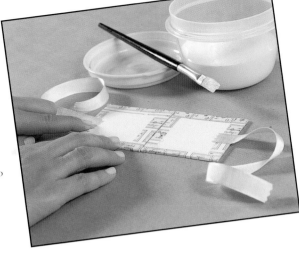

❖6   Lay the contrasting papers right side down. Brush glue from the center out to the edges. Center and adhere the papers to the inside of the cards. Use your thumb or a bone folder to smooth the paper flat.

Match the placement of the ribbons, one on top of the other, so the card will tie properly.

❖7   Place one card on top of the other, with the outside covers facing out and all the edges meeting. Apply glue to the back of the binding strip. Place half of the glued strip evenly on the front left side of the top card. Roll the paper over the edges and adhere it to the back of the card.

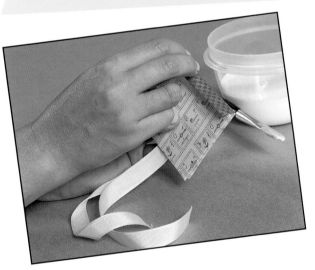

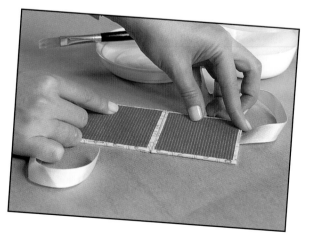

❖8   Open the card flat. Press the left and right edges of the card toward the center to catch the binding strip between the boards. Hold the cards about a minute until the glue sets.

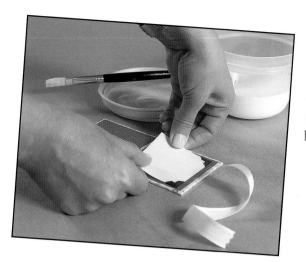

❖9 Place the photo corners on the left and right top corners of the 2 ½" x 2 ½" (6.5 cm x 6.5 cm) writing paper. Apply glue to the back of the corners, center them, and press them onto the inside of the card.
Slide the paper out and repeat the procedure with the bottom corners.

❖10 Make a collage on the front cover with complementary papers. Glue a baby photo for a final layer over the collage.

Variations

For more sophisticated photo mailers, make the paper and the binding all the same color. Add a button that closes the photo mailer with string. Simply glue the button to the top of a glass bead that is then glued to the card. The bead gives the button height to wrap the string around the base.

Keepsake Photo Mailer

T ailor this versatile card to suit almost any occasion. Measure the foam core and outside paper to make the window, then remove the window. Cover the foam core and line the window frame with paper. Glue a piece of paper or a photograph behind the window to serve as a backdrop for your object. Cover the other piece of foam core, then bind the two pieces together. Add picture corners and decorate the window.

Materials

- Two pieces of ¼" (.5 cm) foam core, 4" x 5" (10 cm x 13 cm)
- Two pieces of decorative paper for the outside, 5 ½" x 6 ½" (14 cm x 16 cm)
- Two pieces of decorative paper for the inside, 3 ¾" x 4 ¾" (9.5 cm x 11.5 cm)
- Strip of paper for window lining, ¼" x 7" (.5 cm x 18 cm)
- Piece of card stock or firm paper for behind the window, 3 ½" x 4 ½" (8.5 cm x 12 cm)
- Piece of decorative paper, photograph, or image for the window, 2" x 2 ½" (5 cm x 6.5 cm)
- Piece of paper for the binding strip (use the same paper as on the outside), 4" x 2" (10 cm x 5 cm)
- Object for the window and four picture corners
- T-square
- Eraser
- Craft knife
- Metal ruler
- Pencil
- PVA glue
- Glue brush
- Bone folder
- Cutting mat

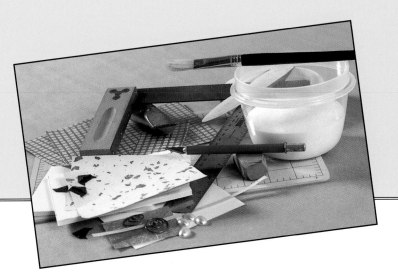

❖ **1** Lay one piece of the foam core on your work surface. Measure and mark with the pencil 1 ¼" (3 cm) from the left and right edges, then measure and mark 1 ½" (4 cm) from the top and bottom edges. Make straight lines with the T-square at the marks to form the shape of the window. Use the T-square as a guide as you cut out the window with the craft knife.

Cut the foam core several times before moving the ruler to ensure that the blade is all the way through.

Draw arrows on the paper and the foam core to use as placement guides.

❖ **2** Make a line ¾" (2 cm) from all edges on the back of the outside paper. Position the foam core within the lines. Hold the foam core in place and use the pencil to trace around the inner edges of the window. Center the piece of card stock under the window and trace around the inner edges of the window again.

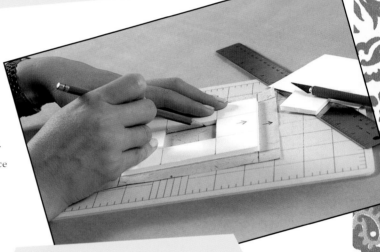

Cut from corner to corner for clean edges.

❖ **3** Remove the foam core and the card stock. On the outside paper, measure ½" (1 cm) from each side of the window outline to form a smaller square. Use the metal ruler and craft knife to cut out the inner square. Then cut a diagonal from each window corner to the corner of the inner square to create flaps.

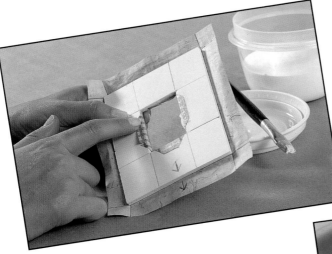

❖4 Apply glue to the back of the outside paper. Center the foam core on the paper within the marked lines and adhere it. Turn the foam core over and smooth the paper with your hand. Pull the flaps gently through the window in the foam core toward the back of the card.

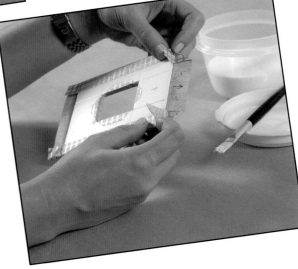

❖5 Apply glue to the left and right flaps along the length of the card. Fold the flaps over the edges and adhere them to the foam core. Glue only as far as the top and bottom edges of the foam core. Glue the paper between the folded flaps at the corners onto the top edge of the foam core.

❖6 Glue the back flap over the top edge toward the front flap. Apply glue and fold both flaps over the top edge toward the back of the foam core. Repeat these steps at the bottom edge of the card.

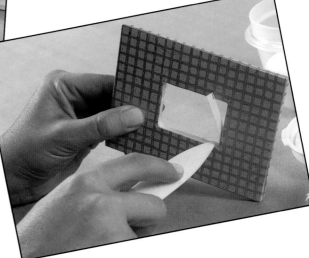

❖7 Apply glue to the back of the ¼" (.5 cm) paper strip. Insert the paper strip at the lower left corner and along the edges of the window. Push it into the corners tightly for an accurate fit. Trim any excess. Use the bone folder to work the paper into the corners and smooth the edges.

Check the length of the paper strip to make sure it fits before applying the glue.

❖**8** Center and glue the 2" x 2 ½" (5 cm x 6.5 cm) window paper onto the card stock over the pre-traced square. Apply glue to the front of the card stock around the window paper. Adhere the front of the card stock to the back of the foam core, so that the window paper appears in the window.

❖**9** Apply glue to the back of the inside paper. Center the paper over the card stock on the foam core and adhere it. Smooth the paper flat with your hands. Create the other side of the card following the previous steps, eliminating the construction of the window.

❖**10** Place one side of the card on top of the other, with the inside papers facing each other. Apply glue to the back of the binding strip. Put half of the glued strip on the front left side of the top card. Pull the other half of the binding strip around the foam core edges to the outside edge of the bottom card.

❖**11** Open the card and lay it flat with the outside covers facing down. Press the right and left edges of the card toward the center to catch the glued strip between the two pieces of foam core. Let the glue set for about a minute. To finish the card, add the picture corners (see the instructions given for the Basic Photo Mailer) and your window object.

H·a·n·d·m·a·d·e E·n·v·e·l·o·p·e·s

*Y*ou can make an eye-catching envelope to complement your handmade card. Envelopes are quick and easy to make using materials that you probably already have around the house: last year's calendars, shopping bags, magazine covers, posters, or handmade paper. The basic envelope shape is just four flaps surrounding a middle rectangle. Once you become familiar with the shape, you can adapt it to accommodate cards of every shape and size. Experiment with the flaps by cutting them into longer, curved, or notched shapes. Or attach the side flaps on the outside of the envelope instead of on the inside. Whatever shape you choose to make, have fun. And don't worry about sending a handmade envelope through the mail; the post office will accept it.

H·a·n·d·m·a·d·e E·n·v·e·l·o·p·e
I·n·s·p·i·r·a·t·i·o·n·s

The simplest way to seal an envelope is with glue, but you can also punch a hole through the top flap and close it with a string or ribbon. Sew the side flaps or the edges of the envelope together with different colors of thread. Use cutouts from magazines or catalogs to create collages. Line the inside with a collection of postage stamps, newspaper comics, or astrological charts. Rubber stamps are great for adding printed images or patterns. However you choose to design your envelope, it will be happily received.

Glue a piece of ribbon along the top flap or sew on buttons for clasps.

To ensure your handmade envelope will fit together, use precise measurements marked with a sharp pencil. Write lightly—any marks you make on the paper will most likely be seen on the finished product.

Easy Handmade Envelope

Using the card to be enclosed in your handmade envelope as a guide, add 4 ½" (11 cm) to the length and 2" (5 cm) to twice the width. To make a pattern, trace lines out from all four edges of the card. The lines divide the paper into five sections: the top flap, main body, bottom flap, and side flaps. Make crisp folds on each line because refolding will leave creases on the outside of the finished piece.

Materials

- Scrap paper for the envelope pattern
- Decorative or solid-color paper for the finished envelope
- Craft knife
- Metal ruler
- Pencil
- PVA glue
- Glue brush
- Bone folder
- Cutting mat or dense cardboard

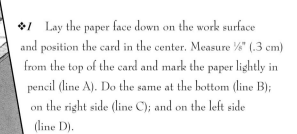

❖1 Lay the paper face down on the work surface and position the card in the center. Measure ⅛" (.3 cm) from the top of the card and mark the paper lightly in pencil (line A). Do the same at the bottom (line B); on the right side (line C); and on the left side (line D).

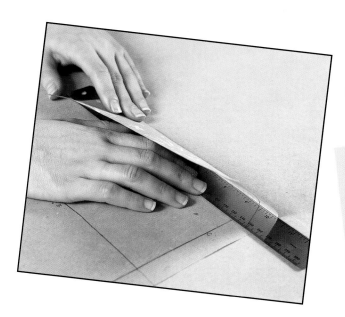

❖2   Remove the card. Place the metal ruler on line A and fold down to make the top flap. Crease the fold with your thumb or the bone folder.

If your enclosed card is a standard size, such as 4" x 6" (10 cm x 15 cm) or 5" x 7" (13 cm x 18 cm), take apart a standard envelope and use it as a pattern.

❖3   Place the metal ruler on line B and fold the paper up to make the bottom flap. Crease the fold.

❖4   Unfold lines A and B. Use the metal ruler to fold lines C and D toward the center of the paper. Crease the folds. You now have the basic shape of the envelope.

❖5   Position the metal ruler on a diagonal at a 45-degree angle through the intersection of lines A and C. For sharp corners and crisp lines, cut from the intersection of the folds out to the edge of the paper.

❖**6**   Position the metal ruler on a diagonal at a 45-degree angle through the intersection of lines A and D. Cut from the intersection to the edge of the paper.

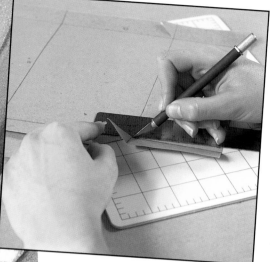

❖**7**   At the top edge of the paper, measure and mark ¼" (.5 cm) to the left of line C (toward the center). Place the ruler on a diagonal through the intersection of lines A and C to the ¼" (.5 cm) mark. Cut from the intersection to the mark.

❖**8**   As in the previous step, measure and mark ¼" (.5 cm) to the right of line D (toward the center). Place the ruler on a diagonal through the intersection of lines A and D and cut from the intersection to the mark.

❖**9**   Position the metal ruler on a diagonal at a 45-degree angle through lines B and C. Cut from the intersection up to the edge of the paper.

For added decoration, line the inside with contrasting paper. Glue together the wrong sides of two contrasting papers. If the papers begin to warp, put them under a pile of books until the glue dries. Then trace the envelope pattern onto the paper that will serve as the inside of the envelope and construct the envelope.

❖10   Position the metal ruler on a diagonal at a 45-degree angle through lines B and D. Cut from the intersection up to the edge of the paper.

❖11   Place the metal ruler horizontally on line D. Cut from the intersection of line B to the bottom edge of the paper. Repeat on line C.

❖12   Now assemble the envelope. Fold lines C and D. Fold line B. Before you apply glue, make sure all the edges are even and all the folds are crisp. If necessary, trim any edges that extend over the left and right sides. Apply glue to the inside edges of the bottom flap and adhere to the side flaps. Add decorative edging to the flap.

Letter Envelope

The beauty of the letter envelope is that you can write notes, glue or draw in pictures, or paste in a collection of stamps or small objects, then fold it up and send your correspondence in style. Cut the paper and add embellishments before you begin to fold. Then measure and mark the paper at intervals to use as a folding guide. Fold the end edges under to create a flap, and make a slit for the flap to fit into. Or try weaving papers through the flap, as shown in the Woven Ribbon Collage project

Materials

- Piece of handmade or heavyweight paper, 5 ½" x 30" (14 cm x 76 cm)
- Piece of solid or patterned paper, 3 ¼" x 5 ½" (8.5 cm x 14 cm)
- Craft knife
- Metal ruler
- Pencil
- Bone folder
- Cutting mat

❖*1* Measure and lightly mark with pencil 7 ¼" (18.5 cm) and 7 ½" (19 cm) away from the left side of the paper at the top and bottom edges. Use the metal ruler and bone folder to score the fold lines. Begin at the 7 ½" (19 cm) mark to measure the remainder of the paper at 3 ¾" (9.5 cm) intervals. Use the ruler and bone folder to score the fold lines.

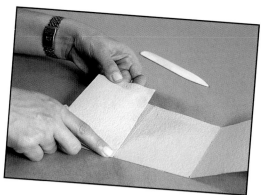

❖2 Fold the right edge of the paper at the first fold line. Align the top edge of the paper with the edge underneath and crease it with the bone folder.

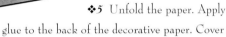

❖3 Turn the paper over. Fold the next section over and crease the paper to make a crisp fold. Repeat to make two more folds.

❖4 Measure and mark 3 ¼" (8.5 cm) from the left edge of the paper. Score and fold the paper. This last section is the envelope flap.

❖5 Unfold the paper. Apply glue to the back of the decorative paper. Cover the envelope flap with the paper. Lay the paper along the fold line and press out to the edge with the bone folder. Trim any excess.

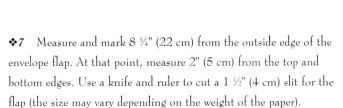

❖6 To finish the envelope flap, measure 2 ½" (6.5 cm) down and 2 ½" (6.5 cm) over from the corners of the flap. Place the metal ruler on the diagonal of each corner at the 2 ½" (6.5 cm) mark. Score and fold the paper.

❖7 Measure and mark 8 ¾" (22 cm) from the outside edge of the envelope flap. At that point, measure 2" (5 cm) from the top and bottom edges. Use a knife and ruler to cut a 1 ½" (4 cm) slit for the flap (the size may vary depending on the weight of the paper).

M·a·k·i·n·g Y·o·u·r O·w·n P·a·p·e·r

Making paper is a magical experience that takes you back to the basics of paper craft. It is fun, easy, and rewarding, and requires only a few household items and readily available art supplies. Once you discover how quickly you can make beautiful paper from scraps of junk mail or papers in your recycling pile, you will find yourself with a growing stack of handmade papers to make into cards, wrapping paper, bookbinding, or any other project.

Most of the supplies you will need for making your own paper are already at hand. You will need a large shallow vat such as a plastic wash basin or a cat litter box, a blender, and the material to make the paper. The best source for this is junk mail and other paper recycling that so easily collects at home. These used papers can be reduced down to paper pulp—a mixture of paper fibers and water—to produce fresh, new sheets of paper. To make existing paper into pulp, remove staples, cellophane, or other miscellaneous materials from the paper. Tear the paper into small pieces and soak in water to soften and break down the fibers. Then put the soaked bits of paper into a blender, with water, to make into pulp.

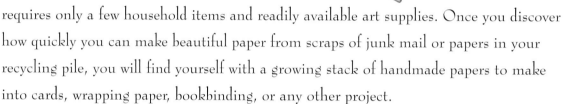

The other supplies you will need to make paper are a deckle and mold, felts, and pressing boards, all of which can be found at artist's supply stores.

The deckle and mold form and determine the size of the final sheet of paper. The deckle looks like a picture frame with a screen covering it. It captures the paper pulp, separating the fibers out from the water as it is removed from the vat. On top of the deckle is the mold, which shapes the sheet of paper. The deckle and the mold are slipped beneath the surface of the pulp in the vat and then lifted out, capturing the paper fibers while allowing the water to drain away.

After you remove the deckle and mold from the vat, you have what is essentially a very soggy piece of paper. To remove the moisture from the paper, press the sheet between felts and boards. The felts absorb some of the extra water, allow you to move the paper in progress from one work station to another, and prevent the paper from sticking to the pressing boards. If you can't find felts, wool blankets cut to size work just as well. Press as much water as possible out of the sheet of paper, then move it to a smooth surface, such as foam core, glass, or Formica, to dry.

Once you understand the basic paper-making techniques, you can easily produce numerous variations and styles of paper. At the pulp stage, add dyes to make colored papers, or mix in found objects such as petals, lace, or string to become an integral part of the paper. Add another sheet of handmade paper, or press shapes into the paper. To turn out larger sheets of paper, use larger deckles and molds and correspondingly bigger vats. If you do not have the room to set up a bigger vat, create larger sheets by overlapping smaller ones. After a sheet of paper has been placed on the pressing board, do not press it, but add another sheet of unpressed paper right next to and touching the first. Continue adding these unpressed sheets until the paper is the size you want, and then place the second felt and pressing board on top of the paper and press as usual. The resulting sheet is a composite of all the smaller sheets you placed together.

How to Make Paper

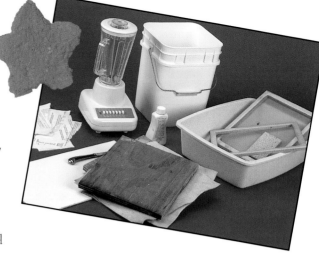

This recipe for navy colored paper is quick, easy, and produces beautiful results. To create a different color paper, simply substitute the blue dye with another color, or after you have made a few blue sheets of paper, add some yellow or red dye to the pulp to make either green or purple sheets of paper. Take your time, have fun, and experiment. The result will be your own unique papers you can use to add a more personal touch to your paper projects.

Materials

- Paper scraps
- Blender
- Water
- Blue dye
- Large shallow vat (large enough to contain deckle and mold)
- 8 ½" x 11" (21.5 cm x 28 cm) deckle and mold
- 2 pieces of felt just larger than the paper you are making
- Pressing boards
- Sheet of foam core or other smooth surface
- Towels and sponges
- Bucket
- Putty or butter knife

❖1 Tear the paper into small pieces, measuring no more than 1" (2.5 cm) square, and place them in the bucket. Add enough water to cover the paper and let it soak overnight to soften the fibers. The next day, put a small handful of the paper pieces into the blender with a little bit of water and blend until the pulp is smooth, with no lumps. It should resemble the consistency of cooked oatmeal. Repeat until all of the soaked paper bits have been made into pulp. Pour it all into the shallow vat and add several tablespoons of the blue dye until you have created a rich, blue-colored mixture.

❖2 Mix enough water into the pulp so that it has a soupy consistency (the more water you add to the pulp, the thinner the sheet of paper will be). Agitate the mixture to ensure an even dispersion of the pulp. Stack the mold on top of the deckle and, beginning at one side of the vat, slip the deckle and mold beneath the surface of the pulp solution in one smooth movement.

❖3   Lift the deckle and mold straight up out of the vat and gently shake them to ensure an even dispersion of the paper pulp. Allow as much water as possible to drain off, and remove the mold from the top of the deckle.

❖4   To prevent the pulp from sticking to the felts, soak them in water and then wring them out. Place one pressing board on the work surface with a piece of felt on top of it. In a quick, smooth motion flip the deckle over onto the felt so that the sheet of paper you are forming is trapped between the screen of the deckle and the felt. With a towel or sponge, press against the screen of the deckle to squeeze out as much water from the pulp sheet as possible. Gently remove the deckle, leaving the pulp sheet on the felt. If the pulp starts to tear as you lift off the deckle, press out more water before continuing.

❖5   Lay the other felt on top of the pulp sheet and the other pressing board on top of that. Press the sheet firmly between the two boards to remove more water. You may find that standing on the boards is the easiest way to do this. Carefully remove the top board and felt.

❖6   Lift the felt that the sheet of paper is on and turn it over onto the foam core, pulp side down. Press the sheet against the foam core and gently peel the felt away from the sheet of paper. If the paper starts to tear, press it back against the foam to remove more moisture before continuing to peel off the felt. Leave the newly formed sheet of paper on the foam for several hours to dry.

❖7   When the edges of the paper sheet start to pull away from the foam core, and the center of the sheet feels dry to the touch, slip a putty or butter knife between the paper and the foam core, and gently pry the paper from the surface.

Paper-Making Tips

To make your own deckle and mold set, use two matching picture frames and enough window screening (available at any hardware store) to cover the opening of one frame. Remove the glass, backing, and stands from the frames so that only the front portion of the frame remains. Wrap the screening around one frame and staple or glue it in place. This frame is now the deckle. Stack the other frame on top of the deckle to use it as the mold for your paper.

Use cookie cutters as molds on top of a deckle to make small, fun shaped pieces of paper to use for invitations or name tags.

To make a thick sheet of paper, add only a little water to the pulp before forming the sheet. For a thin sheet of paper, dilute the pulp considerably with water.

About the Author

Boston-based author and artist Lisa Kerr has been making cards for more than fifteen years. In 1990, her one-time hobby developed into **Monolisa Worldwide**, a successful business that creates cards, blank journals, and photo albums, and distributes them through gift stores in the U.S. and Europe. Kerr has traveled all over the world, gathering unique papers and techniques to use in her card-making. She currently teaches card-making in Boston, Massachusetts. This is her first book.

PRICE 25 CENTS

THE CHICAGO OPERA ASSOCIATION

LIBRETTO

THE ORIGINAL ITALIAN, FRENCH OR GERMAN LIBRETTO WITH A CORRECT ENGLISH TRANSLATION.

Barber of Seville

PUBLISHED BY

FRED. RULLMAN, INC.

THEATRE TICKET OFFICE
111 BROADWAY, NEW YORK
TRINITY BUILDING
THE ONLY CORRECT AND AUTHORIZ

Index

P·a·p·e·r S·a·m·p·l·e·s

The beautiful paper samples provided here are for you to tear out and create cards of your own. The heavier card stock papers can be used as card bases; cut and fold them so that the solid colors lie inside the card—or reverse the pattern for a color surprise inside. Use the smaller images to glue to the card bases. Create card collages with a travel or horticultural theme. Or attach a layer of transparent film, photocopied with a rubber stamp image, over vibrant patterned paper. With the easy card-making instructions inside and these companion papers, you will be well on your way to making original card designs that you can give to your friends and family.

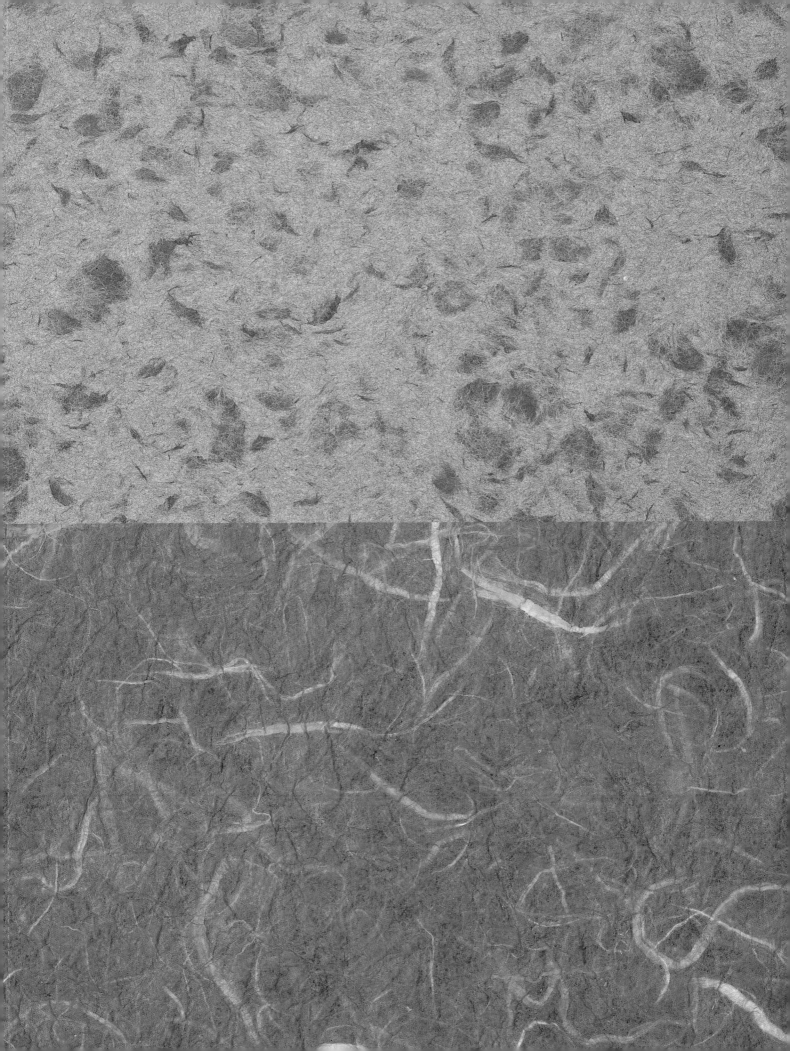

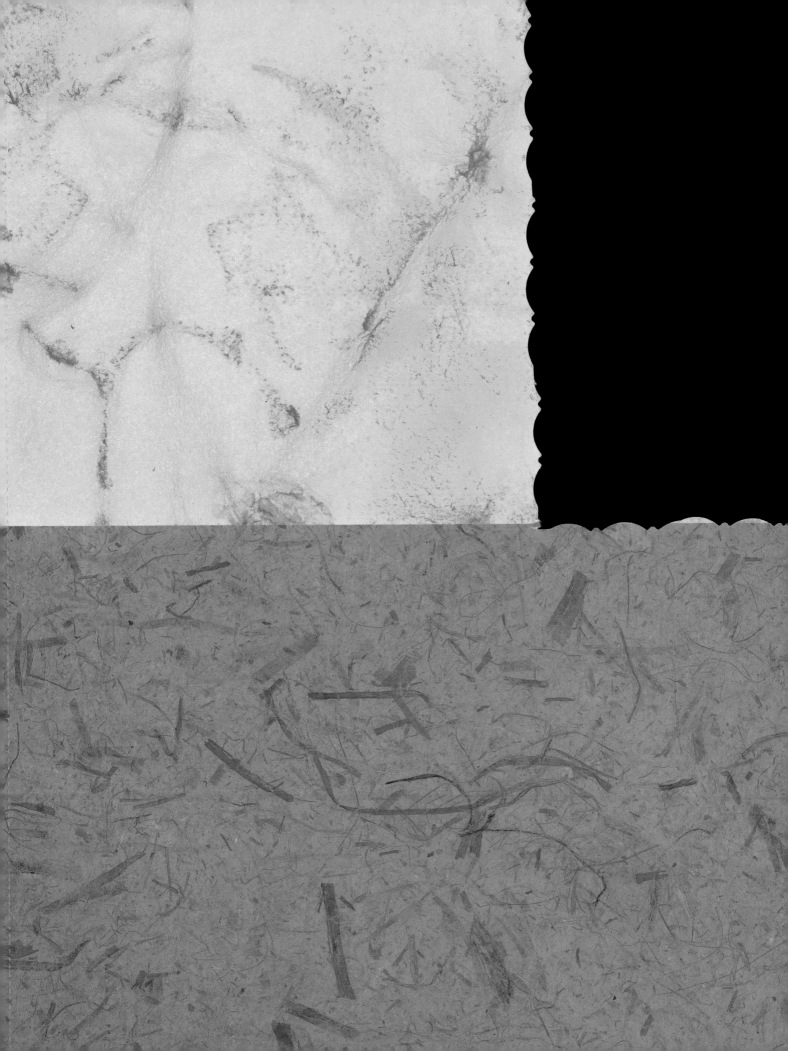

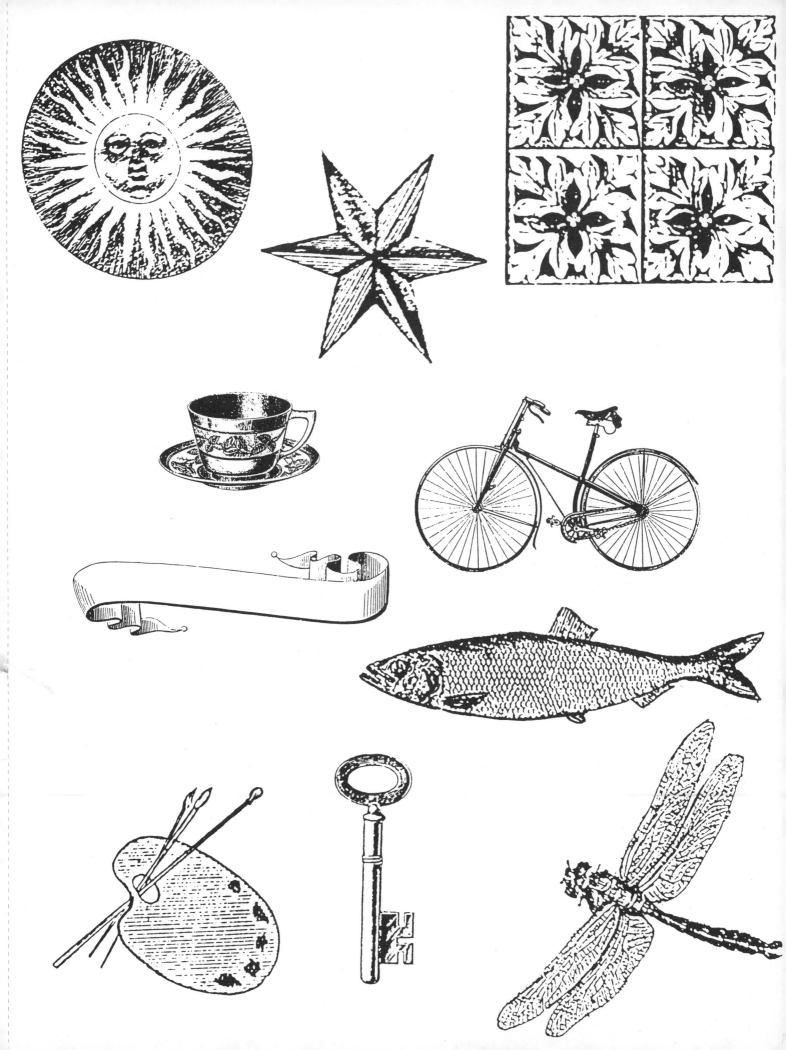